A TRUE STORY
Rev. Aneita Brown

COMING BACK FROM THE DEAD

Scott's
Publishing
CHRISTIAN PUBLISHING

Coming Back From the Dead: A True Story
Rev. Aneita Brown

© 2015 **Rev. Aneita Brown**

Scripture quotations are from the King James Version of the Holy Bible (KJV).

ISBN:978-976-96348-5-5

Rev. Aneita Brown can be reached at:
aneitabrown@yahoo.com

Request for information about this book should be submitted to:
info.scottspublishing@gmail.com

Cover design by: Danever Scott
smgservices81@gmail.com

*This book is dedicated to my seven children;
David Brown, Jennifer Archibald, Trevor Brown,
Andrew Brown, Delroy Brown, Denisha Robinson,
Terryann Scott, and their families.
To the Ambulance Crew that responded to the 911
emergency call and to the staff of Emory Eastside
Medical Center in Snellville.
May God continue to be with you all.*

ACKNOWLEDGEMENTS

Thanks to my Heavenly Father for hearing the cries of the many who prayed for me.

Thanks also to:

» Andrew, my son, who stood in the gap for me and also for the many visits to the hospital.

» His wife, Olivia, for all she did while I stayed with them in Atlanta.

» My daughter, Jennifer, who came from New York to see me, and to her husband, Elton.

» My son, Trevor, for coming all the way from London for three glorious weeks.

» My daughter, Denisha, and her husband, Ralston Robinson.

» My daughter, Terryann, for editing and publishing the contents of this book.

» Her husband, Danever Scott, for doing the cover design of this book.

» My son, David, and his family.

- » My son, Delroy, and his family.
- » Pastor Shawn Bembridge and all the members of Living Waters Christian Centre, Jamaica.
- » My sisters, Veta Charlton, Laura Christian and their husbands, Gilbert Charlton and the late Melbourne Christian who have passed since.
- » My brother, Neville Anderson, and his wife Olive.
- » The late Rev. McLean, who is now deceased, and to his wife, Mrs. McLean.
- » Pamela Leonard, for the many songs she sang to me.
- » All my family and friends for all of your support and prayers on my behalf.

Thank you, and God bless you all.

CONTENTS

INTRODUCTION   *9*

1. MY STORY   13
2. THE FAST   15
3. THE ARRIVAL   19
4. A FUNNY FEELING   23
5. THE REPORTS   25
6. THE MIRACLE   31
7. THE CALLS   33
8. MY REPORT   35
9. LEAVING THE HOSPITAL   41
10. FINAL WORDS   43
11. THE SINNERS PRAYER   47
12. PHOTOS   50

EDITOR'S NOTES   *51*
INSPIRATIONAL READS   *57*

INTRODUCTION

THE OBJECTIVE OF THIS BOOK is to inform all my readers that there is life after death and that the powers of darkness are real, but God's power exceeds all. God has the final say, and that includes in life and death.

When we depart this world, life continues in the next. We will still be able to see, hear, feel, walk, talk and think, and so on. Our senses and our psychological functions will remain with the addition of supernatural abilities and heighten awareness. We will however, receive a new glorified body that will be able to stand in the presence of God and not get weak at His splendor or die if damned. This new body that we all will receive is indestructible. It cannot die, but it lives on forever.

Our God is so powerful. Nothing is impossible for Him to do, for God is Deity.

"The invisible things of Him from the

creation of the world are clearly seen,
being understood by the things that
are made, even His eternal power and
God head; so that they are without
excuse" (Romans 1:20).

We all have to give an account to God after we depart this life. No excuse can save us when we stand before Him. Many of God's people refuse to do what is right because of having too many excuses. People often use the phrase, "God will understand," but will He? The Word of God declares, *"No sin can enter heaven,"* and God has commanded us to be holy like He is, because *"Without holiness, no man can see God."*

God is holy and He has called us to live a holy life. Again, many may ask, "How can someone be holy while living in a sinful world?" Well, my brothers and my sisters, God who knows the beginning from the end would never tell us to do something, if it was impossible.

In the book of Leviticus chapter 20:7, God told His people to sanctify themselves and to be holy as He is; and in verse 26, He said, *"You shall be holy unto me."* This is the life He has called us to and He will have it no other way. We must be separated unto Him if we have hopes of reigning with Him forever.

MY STORY

I am the Senior Pastor of Living Waters Christian Center (LWCC) in Jamaica and I make frequent visits to the United States, as I am also a citizen of the United States of America.

Going to Atlanta Georgia was divinely orchestrated by the Almighty God. Continue reading and you will see why.

It was in June 2011, that I received a phone call that would change my life forever.

I was scheduled for a trip to America where I was to reside with my daughter, Jennifer Archibald and her family when that call came in. My son who lives in Atlanta Georgia, was at the end of the other line. Andrew requested me to visit him instead of going to New York. I spoke with my daughter about the shift and a date was set for me to visit my son on Wednesday, June 8th, 2011. This date was perfect as it was my heart's desire and intention, to attend the wedding of my Assistant Pastor,

Shawn Bembridge, and the beautiful Miss Gillian, only four days before my scheduled visit.

THE FAST

Two weeks before my departure, I was led by God to go on a fast for seven days.
On the first day of my fast, I asked the Lord for a scripture and He gave me Psalm 44: 4-8.

"Thou art my King, O God: command deliverances for Jacob.

Through thee will we push down our enemies: through thy name will we tread them under that rise up against us.

For I will not trust in my bow, neither shall my sword save me.

But thou hast saved us from our enemies, and hast put them to shame that hated us.

In God we boast all the day long, and
praise thy name for ever. Selah."

I repeated this several times throughout each day, so you could say that this was my key passage.

I spent these seven days praying, reading the Word of God and meditating on His Words, from 6:00 a.m. – 6:00 p.m., sometimes until 8:00 p.m., and it was glorious.

Whatever you may be going through right now, I want you to be encouraged. Draw closer to the Lord and ensure you have a personal relationship with God. Try to learn His voice, be obedient to Him and praise Him continually in spite of your circumstance.

"My sheep hear my voice, and I know
them, and they follow me" (John
10:27).

"Howbeit this kind goeth not out but
by prayer and fasting" (St. Matthew
17:21).

Isaiah chapter 58: 6-8 tells us the true meaning of a fast and the results we will see when we obey God's Word.

"Is not this the fast that I have chosen? To loose the bands of wickedness, to undo the heavy burdens, and to let the oppressed go free, and that ye break every yoke?

Is it not to deal thy bread to the hungry, and that thou bring the poor that are cast out to thy house? When thou seest the naked, that thou cover him; and that thou hide not thyself from thine own flesh?

Then shall thy light break forth as the morning, and thine health shall spring forth speedily: and thy righteousness shall go before thee; the glory of the Lord shall be thy reward"
(Isaiah 58:6-8).

May you experience the glory of the Lord as you seek Him in prayer and fasting.

THE ARRIVAL

The day finally arrived for my departure. I was accompanied to the airport by my daughter, Denisha Robinson, and her family.

I checked in and my flight was called shortly after arriving. We boarded the plane and I recall having a funny feeling hard to describe during the flight. The question, "What would happen to me if I took sick on the plane?" rushed through my mind. In a matter of time, we landed at the Hartsfield Jackson International Airport in Atlanta Georgia, USA.

I went through all the preliminaries and met up with my son, Andrew, and my Grandson, Nathan, who were both awaiting my arrival.

We were happy to see each other and we talked all the way home. I answered many questions as Andrew asked about friends and family in Jamaica, and quite odd though not strange, we spoke about persons who have died and were brought back to life. Little did I know that this was the leading of the Holy Spirit to prepare my son for what was to come.

The conversation made our journey seem short and in no time, I was being greeted by my daughter-in-law, Olivia and my other grandson, Caleb, as we made our way into their home. It was a happy moment and everyone was overjoyed. This was my third visit to Atlanta, but it was a special moment because it was my first time meeting the family's newest addition, Caleb.

As soon as I settled in, I had a warm bath, followed by a plate of my favorite meal, chicken, rice, mash potatoes and a lot of vegetables. I was thankful to God for a safe trip and this celebration of thanksgiving continued as Nathan played the Hammond organ while we sang and prayed. It was a joy to see his little fingers find the right keys while his feet just about reached those pedals. I had a full day of fun and laughter so much that we retired late to bed that night. If only I knew what was awaiting me the next day.

Readers, allow me to encourage you. Let us

be ready at all times for God's return or death. No one knows what will happen minutes or hours from now.

I know of a gentleman who came from America to Jamaica to bury his father and he never made it to his dad's funeral. He died days after his arrival in the country.

There is someone else I knew who lived in England for many years. He bought his dream house in Jamaica, then a few days after migrating, he died.

I recall another incident where I visited a young man and his girlfriend who was ill. After praying for them, I encouraged them to get married and he opened a box to show me a beautiful ring. "We have plans to get married," he said. "We will be going to see our Pastor soon." I was so happy for the couple, but the young lady did not live to see her big day; she died. Ladies and gentlemen, the list of stories that are real, go on. Death is certain, but we know not when, therefore, we must be ready.

Be certain you are in right standing with God and stay covered under the blood of Jesus Christ, for there is such a thing as untimely death.

"Be not over much wicked, neither be thou foolish: why shouldest thou die before thy time" (Ecclesiastes 7:17)?

A FUNNY FEELING

It was now Thursday, June 9, 2011, and Andrew was up early for work. I went to his room to say good morning and to wish him a blessed day, then I went back to bed. After a while, the smell from the kitchen told me that it was time for breakfast.

After breakfast, I spent a portion of the day exploring the progress of my grandchildren, those in Atlanta and back in Jamaica.

Suddenly, I began to experience the same funny feeling – hard to describe, that I felt on the plane, so I told Olivia about it.

"Oh mom," she said. "You are jet lagged."

"No, I am not," I replied. "I have traveled many times before and I'm familiar with the feeling of being jet lagged." This feeling was different and it lasted all day.

By now, Andrew was home and I was all refreshed and ready for prayer. My son went upstairs and I noted that the 'funny feeling' was getting worse, so I went to my room to lay on my bed, but I was up in less than a minute for no reason that I could explain (I now know that this was the leading of God). I walked over to the mirror and I was horrified at what I saw. I looked at least twenty years older!

"What is happening to me?" I muttered. I took the bottom plate out of my mouth and instead of lying back down in the room by myself, I returned to the living room and laid on the couch.

"Olivia," I said. "This feeling is getting worse." We continued to converse.

Olivia asked me if I wanted a cup of tea and the next thing I knew, my son was standing over me with his friend, Rev. Mac, along with a sister from his church. I was in Emory Eastside Medical Center.

"What happened?" I asked. This is their report.

THE REPORTS

Olivia: I continued to converse with mom and all seemed well until I offered her a cup of tea without getting a response.

I took note of her and discovered her looking in my direction with a blank expression on her face, so I asked again, "Mom can I get you anything?" She did not reply. "Are you ok? Mom are you ok?" Still, there was no response.

I then observed her glazed eyes and penetrating stare in one direction. I shouted, "Jesus!" in a loud voice, then I screamed for my husband. "Andrew! Andrew! Something is happening to your mom. Come quickly!" In no time, Andrew responded and came running down the stairs speaking in tongues.

At this point, I began to panic. "Mom is not answering me, mom is not answering me."

"Stop!" Andrew refuted. "Don't you see what is happening? This is spiritual warfare!"

Andrew: I was upstairs when Olivia called out in a tone indicating she was in distress. I dropped what I was doing and ran quickly to her assistance. I discovered my mother under a spiritual attack.

As I approached my mother, I observed her eyes as she laid on the couch. Froth escaped the corners of her mouth and there I witnessed her take her last breath. She died before my eyes with her mouth slightly twisted and without warning.

My prior experience as a police officer for over sixteen (16) years have allowed me to witness multiple deaths and this one was no exception. Death was evident, but it was not just anyone, it was no stranger; it was my mother. I hurried my wife to call 911 and her phone's record showed, eight twenty-eight (8:28) p.m. when the call was placed.

Olivia: I quickly dialed 911, then ran over to my neighbor who is a licensed practical nurse in Georgia. We hurried back to my home for my neighbor to offer medical assistance until the arrival of the paramedics. To my amazement, when she saw mom's condition, she started to cry!

Andrew: Suddenly, I felt the power of God came upon me as if I was clothed with His awesome presence. I felt no fear or sorrow, neither the need to panic though tension grew and sadness filled the atmosphere.

My sons sensed it and they began to cry. They knew something was wrong with their grandmother, but the extent of the situation was not understood by them.

On the other hand, something different was taking place on my inside. I was filled with the power of God and I was empowered with divine boldness to take authority over the situation.

I sensed this was an assignment from the kingdom of darkness to take my mother's life before time, so I placed my right hand on her forehead as I rebuked the spirit of death and all other spirits associated with an untimely death. With my hand on my mother's forehead, I declared that she shall not die, but live to declare the works of God. I further declared that this was not of God, for He had spoken into her life and the prophecies were not yet fulfilled. I continued my declarations and I addressed my mother directly by saying, "Mom, you shall live to see the goodness of the Lord in the land of the living." Suddenly my mother gasped for air then returned to a dying state.

The warfare was intense, but I continued to command the enemy to back off in the name of Jesus and I noted clearly that whenever I used the name of Jesus or the blood of Jesus, my mother gasped for air.

This fierce battle continued until the paramedics arrived at 8:38 p.m. They attended to my mother for ten minutes as I continued in warfare. I felt the power of God on me like never before and I had the assurance that everything was going to be fine in spite of how things appeared in the natural.

Outside, my house was dressed with three emergency units and flashing lights — the police department, the fire department, and the ambulance service. I watched as they placed my mother's lifeless body on a stretcher in the back of the ambulance and I sat with her steadfast in prayer. I was later asked to sit in the front of the ambulance and I complied, but the warfare continued. I commanded her to live in Jesus' name and I declared the infallible Word of God over her life.

Olivia: The paramedics worked on mom for about ten minutes and she did not respond. This was dramatic for all of us especially the children.

The doors of the ambulance swung shut and they sped off to the hospital.

Andrew: As I continued in prayer, the driver looked at me, shook his head and waved the palm of his hand from side to side. It became obvious that he had given up on mom as he took the stand to prepare me for the worse. My response? "It is ok. She will live and not die. Everything is going to be fine." Faith spoke.

In that stilled moment, I could hear the emergency crew in the back of the ambulance speaking with someone in the emergency room at the hospital as the siren blazed. She was declared a category one and we were on our way to the Eastside Medical Center in Snellville.

THE MIRACLE

Within ten minutes, the hospital was finally in view. As the ambulance entered the Hospital's driveway, I heard the sweetest voice echoing in my ears. It was the voice of my mother.

In amazement, the ambulance driver looked at me and exclaimed, "This is a miracle! She is alive!" Realizing what he had said, he added, "I guess these things do happen."

Immediately, I developed a keen interest in the questions being asked by the ambulance crew and the answers given by my mom. I was relieved. I could not hold back the smile when I heard them ask, "Who is Andrew?" and she responded, "Oh, he is my son."

The emergency team was already in place and the fact that mom was alive after being dead for thirty minutes continued to bring amazement.

Mom was asked, "Can you move your hands?" Mom raised her hands as if she was in church.

Again she was asked to raise her feet and this she did.

I found out later that after six minutes of the brain not getting oxygen, she should have been a cabbage, not being able to help herself in any way.

[The brain can survive for up to about six minutes after the heart stops. If CPR is started within six minutes of cardiac arrest, the brain may survive the lack of oxygen. After about six minutes without CPR, however, the brain begins to die. Prompt resuscitation allows the physician time to assess and treat the damaged brain, but severe brain damage or a prolonged period without oxygen or glucose causes the death of the brain (science.howstuffworks.com)].

This was truly a miracle. She was wheeled away to emergency room #8 where she was changed and then taken to the MRI department. Several vials of blood were taken without hesitation, for lab work.

THE CALLS

Andrew's phone began to ring off the hook. Calls poured in from Jamaica, London England, New York, New Jersey, and Atlanta. Everyone was concerned and anxious to hear what was happening. As the calls came in, fervent intercession to God from all over went up.

It was a very busy and tiresome period for Andrew and his family, but God sustained them and to Him be all the glory.

"How good and pleasant it is for
brethren to dwell together in unity"
(Psalm 133:1).

There is a well-known Jamaican saying which goes like this: "One han wash de adda," which means, help me when I need help and I'll help you when you need help. You'd be amazed at what we can do when we come together as one.

My readers, God is love and we are to love each other. It was love why Jesus came to earth and gave His life for us.

At 2:00 a.m., I was transferred to the Intensive Care Unit (ICU), room 212. I had pads all over me as I was hooked up to several machines. It looked bad from a natural perspective, but I was confident that God was in control of the situation.

"For we walk by faith, not by sight" (2 Corinthians 5:7).

At 3:30 a.m., the hospital called to inform Andrew of my transfer. That night, Andrew got only two hours of sleep then he was up again to visit me before he went to work that morning.

MY REPORT

I cannot remember speaking to the crew, but I recall two nurses telling me I would be transferred to a hospital ward after some tests were done. I was transferred and many vials of blood were taken for testing.

The night went by quickly and it was now Friday morning. One of the hospital's staff came to my bedside and said, "Mrs. Brown, I am going to do another test. Could you please turn on your left side?"

Immediately as I turned on my side, I saw my spirit out of my body and I realized I was in another world without warning. The place was quite peaceful and there were no trees, no houses, no animals and no mountains. I saw only massive acres of level land as far as my eyes could see, with pure grass. I had no control over where I went, but I was walking super-fast at an abnormal speed, unnatural to mankind. My speed created a wooing sound and another sound effect, hard to describe. I could see, hear, feel and think. I had a different body that I could look at. A new transparent body, but still I was unable to see through it.

Suddenly, I became really dizzy for a few seconds and my spirit went back into my body. My eyes popped open and I saw doctors around my bed along with the young lady who asked me to turn on my left side, standing in the same spot.

"She is back!" one of the doctors exclaimed.

"All I did was to ask her to turn on her left side and she stopped breathing for over a minute!" The lady remarked.

I was dead again, for 60 plus seconds, but God intervened and brought me back to life. God is so merciful and true. Perhaps the reason God allowed me to die a second time was to grant me access to medical proof that I had indeed died. No one can comprehend fully the things that God allows and why, but this was indeed confirmed that I had died, not once, but twice.

I was later told by one of the staff that she heard code blue but had no idea who it was. Later that day when my son came to visit, I felt an itch on my chest and noted two pads – one adjacent to my right breast and the other below my left breast – placed there to restart my heart.

God is awesome. The Word of God is true and it tells us that we will be changed in a moment in the twinkling of an eye and there is life after death.

Man is tripartite. Man has a body, a soul and a spirit. I know without a doubt from my experience that the soul of a man continues to live after death.

Readers, one day you too will die. The big question is, where will you spend your eternity? God loves us so much. He sent His son to die for you and me so that we can have life eternal, but the choice is left to us to accept Him. If you have not yet accepted Jesus as your Lord and Saviour, please do so today. If you are not a Believer, may I challenge you to give your life to Jesus because there IS life after death and no repentance beyond the grave? Doubt will lead you to your doom.

*"Today if you hear His voice, harden
not your heart".*

Two days after, my doctor visited and told me

that I was still in a critical condition. Whenever I looked in the mirror, sickness was my reflection. My face told its own story, but my trust was in God to see me through and I was confident that He would.

I spent six days in ICU taking tests and being monitored closely. The nurses and doctors at Emory Eastside Medical Center in Snellville were very kind and loving. The treatment was exceptional and everyone was courteous and professional. May God bless all the staff and all who assisted from the 911 call was made.

My brothers and sisters, it pays to serve God. After everything was over, I realized that this was a spiritual attack on my life. The strange reflection of myself in the mirror and my horror of looking twenty years older was finally clear.

All my test results came back normal except for my potassium level which was a little low. The devil planned to wipe me out before my time, but God intervened. The powers of darkness are real, but God's power exceeds it all. I'll repeat, it pays to serve God.

During my attack, a fasting service was in session back in Jamaica, and my sister, Laura, saw in the spirit, two witches with my body on an alter poking it with sticks. When the witches realized she saw them, she was threatened. The Lord charged her not to be afraid, but to march around the church three times in praise to Him.

We may not always understand God's ways or how He chooses to work, but it pays to be obedient to Him. My sister marched around the church three times and God opened the eyes of a brother who saw the witches also and what they were doing. God allowed this for confirmation.

Paul reminds us in Ephesians 6:12 that, *"We wrestle not against flesh and blood, but against principalities, against powers, against the rulers of darkness of this world, against spiritual wickedness in high places."* The enemy wants to kill you and me, that is his mission, but Paul exhorts us to keep our whole armor on that we may be able to stand against the wiles of the devil (Ephesians 6: 11). All we need is obedience to God and His Word.

Evil exists, but God has given us authority over the devil and all evil. Psalm 91 says, *"We shall tread upon the lion and adder; the young lion and the dragon we shall trample under foot."* To do so, we must first learn how to abide in the shadow of the Almighty. Where His shadow is, we will find His protection and to be victorious, we must live in His presence at all times.

God will allow things to happen to us, but His Word tells us that He will work all things together for good to them that love Him. He will never leave us nor forsake us for He promised to be with us unto the end of the world and He is here with us every step of the way. He will work ALL things out for our good. We must only believe.

LEAVING THE HOSPITAL

I was discharged on June 14, 2011, on Andrew's birthday and brought home by my daughter-in-law, Olivia.

It was a good feeling to be alive and home again with my family. I was happy to see my grandsons and they were happy to have me home once more. Things were back to normal and my vacation continued in full swing just as before. The only difference was that I now had more family around, a powerful testimony and a new experience; one that will live on forever, one that I will never forget.

*To God be the glory great things He
has done; Amen.*

FINAL WORDS

I am a living proof that there is life after death and I appeal to my readers, choose life today. The bible says, *"Today if you hear His voice, harden not your hearts."* My prayer for you is that you will not only read the words of my testimony in this book, but that you will hear Jesus in my testimony and accept Him today. You have read these words and you have read also the Words of Jesus from the scriptures and I am making an appeal to you right now, please do not harden your hearts against God.

Life continues after death. Even the worms in hell have lost their opportunity of death (Mark 9:44-48). Today you have life, make use of it. Accept Jesus today; ask Him to come into your hearts.

To live is Christ and to die is to gain, but the wages of sin is death. My friend, to die outside of Christ means you are doomed for hell. Life continues even in hell, as the bible tells us that the worms will not die in that place of torment. Death will no longer have dominion over us and hell will be your place of destiny if you should die outside of Christ.

"Where their worm dieth not, and the fire is not quenched.

And if thy foot offend thee, cut it off: it is better for thee to enter halt into life, than having two feet to be cast into hell, into the fire that never shall be quenched:

Where their worm dieth not, and the fire is not quenched.

And if thine eye offend thee, pluck it out: it is better for thee to enter into the kingdom of God with one eye, than having two eyes to be cast into hell fire:

Where their worm dieth not, and the fire is not quenched" (Mark 9:44-48).

Accept Jesus today. Ask Jesus to come into your hearts by saying this simple prayer with me.

THE SINNER'S PRAYER

Father, I am a sinner and I confess my sins to you. Please forgive me for all my sins. Wash me and cleanse me in your precious blood. Come into my heart I pray from this day forward because I choose to serve you as my King. Teach me your ways, and help me to become a better person. Thank you for dying on that cross for me and for accepting me into your family. Thank you for making me a Child of the King, Amen!

If you have just said this prayer, please find a good bible-based church to settle in (ask God for guidance to the right church) and make time to read your bible each day as this is how you will learn and grow in God. Do not forget to pray — prayer is simply talking to God as you would talk to a friend respectably — and keep the faith.

God's coming is soon and as a Child of God, it is your responsibility to keep your hearts pure (St.

Matthew 5:8) and to commit your life entirely to Him. Remember, no sin can enter heaven. Only those with clean hands and a pure heart will see God, so in humility and total obedience, remain spotless before Him.

God bless you all and remember the blessed hope that you now have of the return of our Lord Jesus Christ. Be prepared and be ready to meet Him at all times, for no one knows when He will put in His appearance or when death will strike. Believers, let us be ready. Amen.

"Behold, I shew you a mystery; we shall not all sleep, but we shall all be changed"

(1 Corinthians 15:51).

PHOTOS

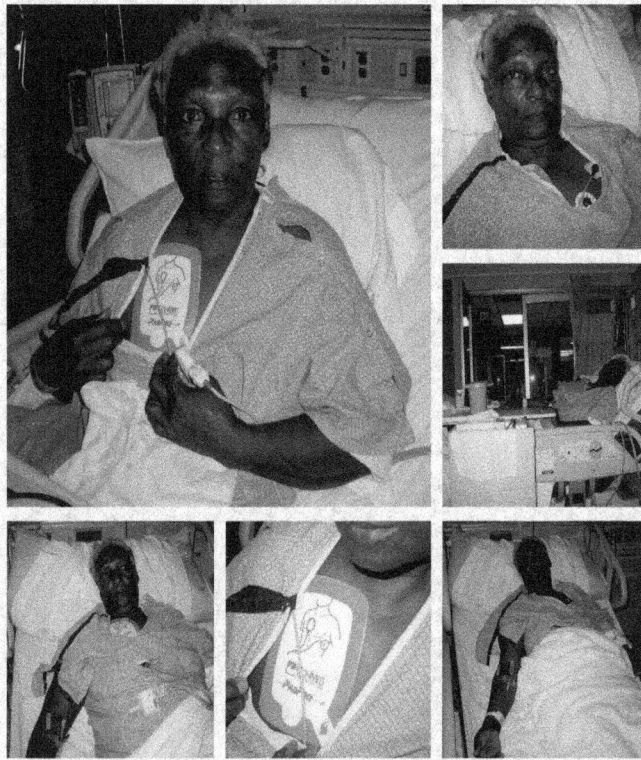

EDITOR'S NOTES

Thank you for downloading this book and for supporting the ministry. By now, you should be able to tell the relation between the Author of this book and me. As the Editor and Publisher, I can confirm that the information shared is real and the story true, of my mother dying and coming back to life, twice.

I can remember the strange thought that pierced my mind, "What if you never see your mom again?" when she left for the airport early that morning without me getting a chance to say goodbye. The news I received of her being rushed to the hospital in an ambulance less than thirty-six hours later, almost made that thought a reality. Though I was instructed to pray, I prayed only what seemed like foolishness to me at that time because I was unable to focus. The only thing I remember saying that made sense was, "Lord have mercy, I did not even get to say goodbye and I want my mommy" (I'm so embarrassed by the latter *smiles*). I became childlike throwing mild tantrums, but I thank God for His mercy and for everyone who God raised up to pray and stand in the gap for my mother.

I enjoy doing what I do and it is readers like you who inspire me to do what I do. If I could make all my books free, I would, but ministry spells work and require a lot of time and resources. My husband and I do ministry together which involves outreach as we have a passion to help others. The more partners we have like you, the broader the scope of our outreach and the more people impacted. If my books have been a blessing to you so far, please continue to read and check out more books I have written below. I encourage you to partner with us and support the ministry through your purchase of any kind. Our goal is to help others, but we can't help them without receiving your help. If you feel the Lord talking to you about purchasing any of my books to assist the ministry, be obedient to His lead, for this is His doing.

To those who were gifted with a free download, do note that this book is also made available in other digital formats. Visit Amazon, Smashwords,

Barnes and Noble, Kobo, iBooks, etc. if you desire another copy in your preferred format, and remember to leave your review.

If you would like your friends to receive a copy of this eBook free, direct them to my website telling them to subscribe to my mailing list. In addition to subscribing, they will receive an additional FREE eBook entitled, Sixty-One Thoughts that can Change Your Life: Wisdom Nuggets, just like you.

If you are not a subscriber, <u>Subscribe</u> to receive updates, new releases, and other freebies (if you have already subscribed there is no need to subscribe again as it will only lead to duplicate emails).

<u>SUBSCRIBE NOW</u> while offer last or visit my website at <u>http://terryannscott1.wix.com/terry-ann-scott</u>

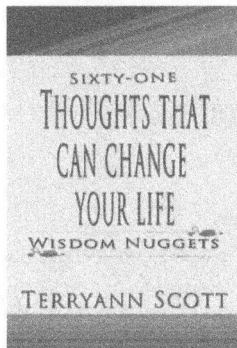

Connect with me on Twitter, Facebook and You-Tube

******

Here is another freebie offering Inner Healing, Personal Development and Spiritual Transformation. Overcoming Obstacles: Hope Devotional

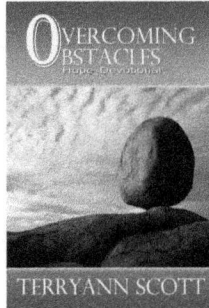

Overcoming Obstacles: Hope Devotional
(Available FREE on popular distribution sites)

Are you struggling with inner fears? Do you feel like giving up? It is never always easy to forgive someone who cost you pain or to step out in confidence after a broken relationship. It's never easy to move past the painful memories that linger, but with a little guide and the right mindset, it can be done.

Every person created here on earth is designed & destined for a unique purpose. Before purpose can be identified & fulfilled, our hearts need to be healed & our minds renewed.

Overcoming Obstacles is an Inner Healing Devotional Guide for those who are emotionally and mentally challenged. It is designed for those who are struggling with their image and self-worth. It offers hope and encourages spiritual healing in practical ways that will lead to healing for the total man.

Overcoming Obstacles consists of fourteen devotionals that may be used daily or weekly as a foundational guide. It is not a complete guide on hope or inner healing, but rather personal insights that will assist the Christian Believer in discovering themselves in God while changing their outlook on life. Further reflections are encouraged. Are you ready for the challenge?

Recommend this free devotional to your family and friends. May God bless you as you partner with us in helping to share the Word of God with others.

******

Reviews are important to every Author. Please submit a review for Hope Devotional HERE. Your reviews help and will assist others in finding this free devotional guide. Don't stop here, but tell your family and friends about this free devotional. This guide may be what they need during difficult times.

******

If you have a Supernatural Encounter you would like to share, please submit your experience(s) to info.scottspublishing@gmail.com along with your byline. Submissions will be collated and published. Your experience matters and can become the agent of change in someone's life today.

******

BOOKS *BY* THE EDITOR

Thank you for your support in purchasing my books.

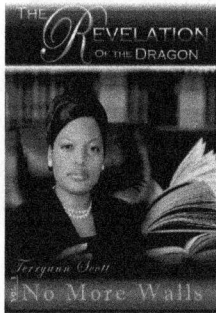

The Revelation of the Dragon: No More Walls
Vol. 1 of "The 'No More' Series"

MY ENTIRE LIFE CHANGED AND YOURS CAN TOO by simply utilizing this powerful warfare strategy that God has released for His people.

"The Revelation of the Dragon: No More Walls," exposes the forces of darkness that is behind the longstanding cycles of disappointments, setbacks, fear, confusion, lack, poverty and so much more.

This revelation came in the most trying and difficult time of my life and I had a rude awakening that led me on a journey of self-discovery and finding God. After my husband and I radically sought God, God stepped in, delivered our family and revealed the culprit that was behind our struggles. I recognized almost immediately that a terrible long-standing cycle of pain, misery, and carry-overs was broken from off our lives with very little effort on our part except by being obedient to God and through maintaining a closer walk with Him.

I am excited about what has transpired in my life and I can hardly wait to get this information into your hands. I pray that Pastors and Leaders will get a copy of this book that they can spread the word within their congregation to impact change.

If you've been experiencing disappointment after disappointment and discouragement after discouragement, or if it seems like progression and succession are leaving you far behind, then *"The Revelation of the Dragon: No more Walls"* is for you.

Discover more about *The Revelation of the Dragon,* as this might very well be the solution to your problems, the answer to your prayers -- the answer that you have been waiting for. I know you will be blessed!

Available on amazon and on other digital retailers.

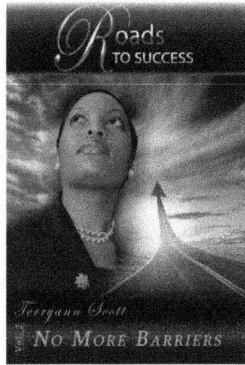

Roads to Success: No More Barriers Vol. 2 of "The 'No More' Series"

Every person has a strong man governing their life and in order to be successful that strong man must first be identified and defeated. In Volume 1, *The Revelation of the Dragon: No More Walls*, Terryann Scott exposes a powerful spirit behind long-standing struggles such as disappointments, dryness, and lack in the lives of people.

In Volume 2, *Roads to Success: No More Barriers*, Minister Scott reveals two hidden paths and five main roads you'll want to travel on for guaranteed success.

Mrs. Scott unfolds the heart of God towards His people while exposing seven Biblical Processes and four Biblical Principles that will transform your life from barrenness to fruitfulness.

In this book you will:

o Learn the seven Biblical Processes and four Biblical Principles for guaranteed success

o Discover how your past can hold you back.

o Identify hidden blocks from your past and learn how to overcome them.

o Discover the heart of God, His promises towards His children and how to acquire them.

o Discover the role of your obedience to God.

o Identify 'roads' to travel on daily for guaranteed success and

o Learn how you can use the law of attraction

by God's design to create the life you've always dreamed of, God's way.

Do not stop here, a new life awaits you! I know you will be blessed.

"Your success in life is not determined by God, but by your obedience to Him"

~ Terryann Scott.

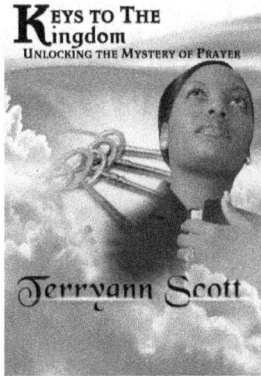

Keys to the Kingdom:
Unlocking the Mystery of Prayer

Why are some prayers answered and not others? Why does a good God allow bad things to happen to people? Why am I praying, but I'm not getting my prayers answered? Is God real? If you are curious about the Mysteries of the Kingdom and how to get your prayers answered, then this book is for you.

In this book, Minister Terryann Scott shares personal stories and testimonies she has obtained through spiritual encounters with Jesus and supernatural revelations given in the spiritual realm.

Just as there are laws that govern the formation of water into ice, so too there are spiritual laws that govern prayer. If these laws are not understood and if the conditions required for prayer are not met, our prayers will not be answered.

I am so excited to be able to share with you what the Lord has taught me on the subject of prayer and Kingdom power. Join me now with this intense read as we take a peek into the supernatural realm to discover, how to get your prayers answered, as we unlock the Mystery of Prayer.

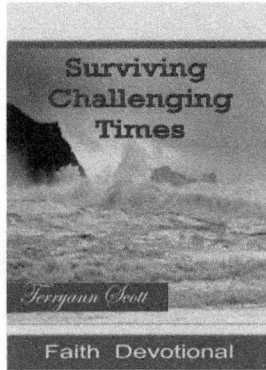

Surviving Challenging Times:
Faith Devotional

Why does God allow bad things to happen to His people? Why is life so challenging and difficult at times? Is God even there? Does He love me and does He care?

These are all questions that are asked when difficult times arise. *Surviving Challenging Times* is a weekly devotional geared to strengthen your Faith and uplift your spirit in God while transforming your thinking. It is designed to inspire, educate, challenge, provoke and motivate a new way of thinking, that you will not only be able to survive challenging times, but also reap the wonderful benefits of surviving faith.

Are you ready for the challenge? Join me on a 21-week journey of exploring, challenging and growing your faith in God.

Hidden Truths: Daily Devotional

Hidden Truths is a daily devotional filled with spiritual wisdom and spiritual insights exposing the hidden works of darkness from the truth of God's Word. Discernment is a crucial part of the Believers-walk with Christ. Everything that glitters is not gold and the Bible tells us that the devil can transform himself as an angel of light. It is, therefore, our responsibility to try every spirit so that we are not deceived.

This devotional is eye-opening, educating, thought-provoking and necessary. It is designed to stimulate the heart of the Believer for a closer walk with God. This is not a complete compilation on the subject, but rather personal insights that will assist the Christian Believer in gaining knowledge while discovering God in a new way.

Further reflections are encouraged through meditation and prayer after reading each devotional guide.

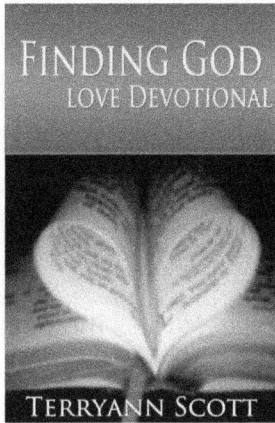

Finding God: Love Devotional

Finding God is about pursuing Him. It is about going after God with all your Heart and discovering Him, especially in hard times. God is almost always discovered through pain, based on the response of the individual challenged and pain can, therefore, be a blessing in disguise when used to touch God.

I discovered God through much heartache and pain (I spoke about this in, *The Revelation of the Dragon: No More Walls vol. 1*). I remember when I thought my life was over and the only person I had left was God. This caused me to experience a rude awakening which brought me closer to Him. I was a Christian for many years, but it was not until I found Him in such a profound way that I realized I was like Peter, walking with God, but not converted.

After my conversion, I noted things changed dramatically with only little prayer but sincere efforts on my part, focusing on God while putting His Words into practice. I was amazed at how much I discovered God, so much that I decided to marry my new found lifestyle with much prayer. That was when I discovered, it is not just in the praying, but the doing. There are many men and women of prayer whose life remains the same because they are hearers of the Word and not doers.

My eyes were immediately opened as I discovered the seriousness of living out the Word of God in obedience and merging that lifestyle with prayer. I got astounding results with a little prayer and by becoming a doer of the Word instead of just a hearer, in comparison to much praying and no results due to lack of practicality. What we do is more important to God than what we pray and how long we pray. God honors our lifestyle and obedience above our prayers.

God is a practical God and if you need results, follow me for a few days on this journey throughout our Love Devotional Guide. Are you ready to discover His presence?

MUSIC

Love listening to Music?

Check out this soul-stirring Gospel Collection of fifteen songs that will leave you wanting more. The heartfelt worship will draw you into the presence of God causing you to crave Him, while the praises capture your mind and soothe your soul encouraging you to trust God.

The words of the songs will minister and the anointing that these songs carry will lift you higher to another level. Well then, don't just take my word for it. Go see for yourself by clicking on the link below.

New Level *by* Danever Scott
(Minister, Music Producer, Gospel Artiste)

COMING SOON:

Becoming a Better You: Heal Your Soul, Heal Your Life

When Two Hearts Become One: Formula for a Successful Marriage

The Power of a Free Spirit: No More Baggage Volume 3